PRAYING THE
KING'S AGENDA

DAYS OF FOCUSED PRAYER

Dana Olson

21 Days of Focused Prayer: Praying the King's Agenda

Written by Dana Olson

© Copyright 2019 Converge. All rights reserved.

Scripture reference: Unless otherwise noted, all Scripture references are from the English Standard Version.

Introduction 3

Day 1 – "Let there be light" 6

Day 2 – "Follow me" 8

Day 3 – "Come to me" 10

Day 4 – "I am the bread of life" 12

Day 5 – "Take up your cross and follow me" 14

Day 6 – "Love the Lord your God" 16

Day 7 – "Love your neighbor as yourself" 18

Day 8 – "Pray without ceasing" 20

Day 9 – "Don't be anxious" 22

Day 10 – "Love your enemies" 24

Day 11 – "Blessed are those who hear the word of God and keep it" 26

Day 12 – "Worship in spirit and in truth" 28
Day 13 – "Lay up treasures in heaven" 30
Day 14 – "What God has joined together let no man separate" 32
Day 15 – "Render to Caesar the things that are Caesar's" 34
Day 16 – "I and the Father are one" 36
Day 17 – "I will make you fishers of men" 38
Day 18 – "Make disciples of all nations" 40
Day 19 – "You will be my witnesses" 42
Day 20 – "I am the way, the truth and the life" 44
Day 21 – "King of Kings and Lord of Lords" 46
About 48

Praying the King's Agenda

What is the King's Agenda? Imagine a grand, powerful and attention-grabbing voice. Whose voice do you think of? Our answers would probably be somewhat generational. Older ones might think of Paul Harvey. His distinctive voice and unique rhythm and cadence, with dramatic pauses, jumped right out of the radio. "And that's (pause, pause) the rest of the story. (Pause, pause, even more pause) Good day."

Fan of Star Wars? "Luke, I am your father." Darth Vader was vocalized by the renowned James Earl Jones, whose voice certainly commanded attention. When Darth spoke, we shivered. Baseball fan? Certain voices come through the radio and are familiar friends (does anybody listen to the radio anymore?). Vin Scully comes to mind, or Red Barber, or for me as a boy in Pennsylvania, Bob Prince. Alas, I'm dating myself again. Who are the voices of the younger generations?

Whoever you think of as The Voice, not singing but speaking, a voice that makes you take notice, imagine that voice reading these words from the Book of Revelation 19:11-16:

"Then I saw heaven opened, and behold, a white horse. The one sitting on it is called Faithful and True, and in righteousness he judges and makes war. [12] His eyes are like a flame of fire, and on his head are many diadems, and he has a name written that no one knows but himself. [13] He is clothed in a robe dipped in blood, and the name by which he is called is The Word of God. [14] And the armies of heaven, arrayed in fine linen, white and pure, were following him on white horses. [15] From his mouth comes a sharp sword with which to strike down the nations, and he will rule them with a rod of iron. He will tread the winepress of the fury of the wrath of God the Almighty. [16] On his robe and on his thigh he has a name written, King of kings and Lord of lords."

There is no question who this horse-riding champion is — it's Jesus Christ. This is a future vision of Christ's return to earth. He will come as a victorious Conqueror; a faithful, true and righteous Judge; a merciful Savior (the robe dipped in the blood of the cross); the Word of God; and, yes, King of kings and Lord of lords.

Jesus is the King of kings. He is the Lord of lords. When a king speaks, his subjects listen. When a lord (master) sets the agenda, that agenda is followed to a T.

The great news for us as Jesus-followers is this: All Jesus reveals about himself and all he commands of us in his word is for our good. We have a kind, caring and benevolent King who wants joy, hope, rest and contentment for us both now and forever. He is not a killjoy. His yoke is easy and his burden is light. He's no slave driver or despot. His commands are not about his ego. He laid down his life for God's people, and he has a plan for our eternal happiness. He is a gracious giver of many gifts.

One of these is prayer. Jesus invites us to pray often and makes magnificent promises about prayer (see Matthew 7:7-11). The question is how do we know what to pray for? How do we know when our prayers are healthy, good, Christ-honoring and not self-centered or wrongly motivated (James 4:3)?

That's why praying the agenda of Jesus Christ himself is a wise and healthy practice. Pray the King's Agenda. That same Jesus who is King of kings has communicated so much to us in his word. He's told us about himself. And he's told us what he commands. When we pray truth about our Savior and pray according to his commands, we must be on the right track, no? This is praying the King's Agenda: Take what Jesus has revealed and pray it back to him. These 21 Days of Focused Prayer won't begin to exhaust all that the Scriptures reveal about Jesus or all that comes from him. But it's a wise start. And it sets a pattern you can continue.

Each day, we invite you to: Read a brief passage with a truth about Jesus or a command from him. Notice some details from the passage, to aid in understanding. Think about it. What does this imply for me today? How will this impact my day (my week, my month, my life)? Pray. We will offer a suggestion for a prayer starting point, but feel free to "build your own" prayer from there. Want to reflect more on what the Scriptures say about these things? Additional Bible passages are offered for deeper thought. Finally, take a moment and respond personally to each day's truth and prayer opportunity. What is the King, Jesus Christ, saying to me personally through his word today? How can I share it with someone who needs Jesus?

Praying the King's Agenda is simply another way of saying, "Hear what the Lord Jesus has to say to you from the Bible, and pray about that in response." It is allowing your Savior, Jesus, to set your prayer agenda. It is praying the Bible.

For thousands of years new generations of Christian believers have learned the depth and power of praying Scripture. It has transformed untold numbers of Christians. The extraordinary Martin Luther (whose treatise on prayer influenced our two previous 21 Days of Prayer booklets, thanks to Gary Rohrmayer), George Muller, Hudson Taylor, on and on the list could go. Want to grow a more focused, powerful and meaningful prayer life? Learn to pray Scripture. Want to know where to start? Start with the agenda of Jesus Christ. Pray the King's Agenda.

PRAYING THE
KING'S AGENDA

_____
Name

_____
Start Date

DAY 1

Praise the Creator who said, "Let there be light," and there was light.

John 1:1-5
In the beginning was the Word, and the Word was with God, and the Word was God. ² He was in the beginning with God. ³All things were made through him, and without him was not any thing made that was made. ⁴ In him was life, and the life was the light of men. ⁵ The light shines in the darkness, and the darkness has not overcome it.

Notice
One of the most extraordinary things said about Jesus in the Gospels is noted in John 1:3: "Without him was not any thing made that was made." Think about that for a moment. The world we live in, including all the universe, the billions of stars, the sun and moon, the continents and oceans, the majestic peaks and Grand Canyon; the eagles that fly, the lions that roar, the fabulous colorful flowers and the fish of the sea — Jesus Christ created all. The same Jesus who died on the cross for us, who said, "Follow me," who healed the sick and the blind and raised Lazarus — created your world. He created you.

Think about it
When you pray to God the Father, in the name of Jesus Christ, you are praying to the God who called every star by its name and placed them in orbit. That same God knows the physics behind a major-league curveball and the anatomy that keeps your heart beating in your chest. When God said, "Let there be light" and there was light, Jesus Christ was there (Genesis 1:3). What implications does that have for your worship?

A prayer of praise
"I praise you, God, for you not only created the universe, but you created me and breathed the breath of life into my lungs. I praise you that I am fearfully and wonderfully made. I praise you for giving me life, breath and every good and perfect gift that makes my life possible. It thrills my soul to know my Savior, Jesus Christ, the King of kings, was there when the planets and stars were set in motion.

God, I exalt you as Creator and submit my life to you to fulfill every good work you have planned for me today. I know nothing is impossible with you, and so I will live today in the great joy and hope of being a child of the King. May every step I take today be to the praise and glory of Jesus Christ, the King of kings and Lord of lords, who is my King. I will live the King's Agenda today. In Jesus' name, amen."

To read more of God's word
Genesis 1, Psalm 148, John 1

Write a personal response to the King's Agenda

Submit to the One who said, "Follow me."

Luke 5:27-32
After this he went out and saw a tax collector named Levi, sitting at the tax booth. And he said to him, "Follow me." ^{28} And leaving everything, he rose and followed him. ^{29} And Levi made him a great feast in his house, and there was a large company of tax collectors and others reclining at table with them. ^{30} And the Pharisees and their scribes grumbled at his disciples, saying, "Why do you eat and drink with tax collectors and sinners?" ^{31} And Jesus answered them, "Those who are well have no need of a physician, but those who are sick. ^{32} I have not come to call the righteous but sinners to repentance."

Notice
Consider whom Jesus was calling when he called Levi (more commonly known as Matthew). A tax collector, Levi was considered an outcast by the Jews of the time, who despised their Roman occupiers. The system of collection led to deep suspicions of theft — collecting more than needed to pad one's own pocket. But that's just the kind of person Jesus came to seek, a sinner in need of saving. I qualify. You qualify. We all do. And as Jesus called Levi, he also calls us.

When Jesus said to Levi, "Follow me," that's just what the tax collector did. He left everything, got up from the tax booth and followed Jesus. He then threw a big feast for his new Master. Following Jesus requires submission to him. He wants no "halfway" disciples. Jesus is Lord and King. Following him may require leaving behind some stuff. It certainly means a change of direction. Jesus wants to come to your house, dine with you — in fact, live with you — and lead you.

Think about it
Following Jesus involves submitting to a new Master. A new King is on the throne of your life. What a beautiful, new direction our lives take. Our new King created the universe, came to earth to save us and offered his life on the cross in our place. And he rose from the dead to lead us to his eternal kingdom, the new heavens and new earth. Jesus guides us through life's pain and challenges, hurts and disappointments and blessings, while filling our lives with purpose, hope and joy. To follow may mean short-term pain, but the long-term benefits are fabulous.

A prayer of submission
"Father in heaven, today I acknowledge Jesus Christ is my Master. He's my King. I submit my day, my week, my life to him. I am filled with joy, for I know any short-term pain will bring eternal benefit. I yield my every circumstance to your loving lordship and leadership in my life. Like Levi in the Gospel of Luke, I leave my stuff behind to wholeheartedly follow Jesus, knowing he has my well-being in view. Take me, Father, for I am yours. In Jesus' name, amen."

To read more of God's word
Luke 5, Psalm 139

Write your personal response to the King's Agenda

Find rest with the One who said, "Come to me."

Matthew 11:27-30
All things have been handed over to me by my Father, and no one knows the Son except the Father, and no one knows the Father except the Son and anyone to whom the Son chooses to reveal him. ²⁸ Come to me, all who labor and are heavy laden, and I will give you rest. ²⁹ Take my yoke upon you, and learn from me, for I am gentle and lowly in heart, and you will find rest for your souls. ³⁰ For my yoke is easy, and my burden is light."

Notice
A yoke was a wooden frame for joining oxen to do the heavy lifting in a hard job. It formed the tractor of Jesus' day to work the fields or haul a huge load. For the Jews of Jesus' day, the law had been turned into a heavy burden, a crushing yoke, impossible to fulfill. Jesus offered a better way, walking with him by faith. He knew God the Father and the love of the Father, and he knew that to walk with God should give rest, not a crushing load.

Think about it
Are you tired? Life can be hard. From cancer to career, from romance to ridicule, from disappointment to delight, life is no picnic. In need of rest? Aren't we all? Let Jesus take the weight off your shoulders. Let Christ lighten your load. He doesn't promise all your problems will disappear; he does promise to walk with you through all of them — to be your Shepherd, Guide and Friend. And he has no plan to make religion a crushing yoke for you. Rather, he offers the joy of forgiveness, freedom and fellowship for life's journey and then — his eternal kingdom. He welcomes you into his church, his family, his body and says, "Let me give you rest. Let me lighten your load. Let me lead you on the grand adventure of changing the world."

One more thing
Perhaps you have found rest through trusting in Jesus Christ. But you know of others who are deeply burdened and in need of Jesus' help. Write down a few names here and pray for them.

A prayer for rest

"Heavenly Father, I want the rest that comes from walking with Jesus. I need it. Please take the heavy load of all that makes my life hard and carry them for me (tell God what those things are, if you'd like to do so). And I pray not only for myself, but for others who feel the crushing burden of life weighing them down. (Mention those people by name here.) Thank you, Father, for the promise of rest. Thank you for shouldering my burdens for me. And thank you not only for rest today, but for the great promise of everlasting rest through Jesus Christ, amen."

To read more of God's word
Joshua 1, Hebrews 4

Write a personal response to the King's Agenda

Trust in the One who said, "I am the bread of life."

John 6:35-40
Jesus said to them, "I am the bread of life; whoever comes to me shall not hunger, and whoever believes in me shall never thirst. ³⁶ But I said to you that you have seen me and yet do not believe. ³⁷ All that the Father gives me will come to me, and whoever comes to me I will never cast out. ³⁸ For I have come down from heaven, not to do my own will but the will of him who sent me. ³⁹ And this is the will of him who sent me, that I should lose nothing of all that he has given me, but raise it up on the last day. ⁴⁰ For this is the will of my Father, that everyone who looks on the Son and believes in him should have eternal life, and I will raise him up on the last day."

Notice
Hunger and thirst are cravings common to all people. Jesus acknowledges here that each of us has a spiritual craving as well as a physical one. Deep inside us we have a gnawing need for something more. People try many things to quell that inner spiritual gnawing hunger and thirst, from food to sex to success to money to power and on and on the list goes. But nothing satisfies. Jesus came to offer what alone will satisfy our hunger — himself. "Believe in me. Trust in me. I am the bread of life that you need to sate your inner thirst." To trust in Jesus is to receive the gift of eternal life. Jesus not only satisfies for the here and now, but for all eternity.

Think about it
What do you believe in to meet your inner craving? Has your ravenous inner hunger been satisfied? Have you learned to chew on the Jesus bread? If you are reading this, you likely have trusted in Jesus Christ and are walking with him. What a gift you have received. Is anything currently diverting you from your walk with Jesus? Is anything tempting you to turn aside from the path of Christ-centered faithfulness to the world's carnival? Beware of that constant temptation. That bread will not satisfy.

A prayer for eating the Jesus bread
"My Father, what an extraordinary gift you have given — your Son. Thank you for sending us the Bread of Life. By your grace and the Holy Spirit, help me to keep walking with Jesus. Keep me from straying off the path of faithfulness and wandering after distractions that will never satisfy. I want to keep trusting in Jesus no matter what. And I pray for my family, my friends, our church — God, keep us trusting, keep us believing, keep us hoping in the One True Source of Life, Jesus. Keep us following the Leader you have given us, the Bread of Life, King Jesus. Help me today to point others to him. Amen."

To read more of God's word
Exodus 16, Psalm 78, I Corinthians 11:23-26

Write a personal response to the King's Agenda

Submit to the One who said, "Take up your cross and follow me."

Luke 9:22-27
"The Son of Man must suffer many things and be rejected by the elders and chief priests and scribes, and be killed, and on the third day be raised." 23 And he said to all, "If anyone would come after me, let him deny himself and take up his cross daily and follow me. 24 For whoever would save his life will lose it, but whoever loses his life for my sake will save it. 25 For what does it profit a man if he gains the whole world and loses or forfeits himself? 26 For whoever is ashamed of me and of my words, of him will the Son of Man be ashamed when he comes in his glory and the glory of the Father and of the holy angels. 27 But I tell you truly, there are some standing here who will not taste death until they see the kingdom of God."

Notice
The cross and the Easter resurrection of Jesus are the very heart of our gospel. When our King Jesus died for us, he opened wide for us the door to his kingdom. It is the King's Agenda for us now to turn from self-directed living to cross-centered living ("deny himself and take up his cross daily and follow me"). The temptation Jesus describes here is to go hard after this world's agenda, whatever that might be, even gaining it but, in the process, losing one's self. We might "gain" something temporarily, like money, power, earthly pleasure or success, but if our soul is lost, if eternity with Jesus is lost, woe to us. Instead, our King says, "Follow me."

Think about it
Our sin nature is selfish. When we repent and trust Jesus, the King calls us to live a cross-centered life of walking with him. We turn in a new direction and submit to the King's Agenda. What is that agenda? Certain things are common to all of us: following the clear commands of the King from Scripture, fellowship with the church (his body), using our spiritual gifts. Others are more individual: what our gifts are and how we use them, where we live, who we relate to in discipleship or service. How are you submitting to the King's Agenda for your life?

A prayer of submission to the King
"It amazes me, Father, that today I can walk with King Jesus in a life of joyful service to you. Thank you for giving me this life, with a place and people, a context for using my gifts and time and energy for your kingdom agenda. Help me today to notice the opportunities you place in front of me. Help me to serve others with gladness, with the strength you supply me, communicating the love of Jesus. Take my life, Father, and let it be set apart to you and your agenda for the benefit of others and the building up of your kingdom. In Jesus' name, amen."

To read more of God's word
Psalm 27, Romans 12, I Peter 4

Write a personal response to the King's Agenda

DAY 6

Love the One who commanded, "Love the Lord your God."

Matthew 22:34-40
But when the Pharisees heard that he had silenced the Sadducees, they gathered together. [35] And one of them, a lawyer, asked him a question to test him. [36] "Teacher, which is the great commandment in the Law?" [37] And he said to him, "You shall love the Lord your God with all your heart and with all your soul and with all your mind. [38] This is the great and first commandment. [39] And a second is like it: You shall love your neighbor as yourself. [40] On these two commandments depend all the Law and the Prophets."

Notice
People love discussions about "who is the greatest" or "which is the greatest." Sports radio loves a raging "G-O-A-T" debate, as in the "greatest of all time." MJ or LeBron? The Babe or Mickey Mantle? Want to start an argument? Ask a group of Americans which is the most important right of the Bill of Rights.

In this exchange about the law, religious leaders are trying to cause Jesus trouble. It's the GOAT question applied to God's law, the Torah. Which of God's commands is the greatest? Jesus answers brilliantly. Who can argue? After all, every Jewish child was taught to love God with their entire being as a "first principle" (see Deuteronomy 6:5). And now Jesus teaches us the same. Love God totally: emotional self, spiritual self, intellectual self — love him with your entire being.

Think about it
What do you think it means to love God with your entire being? To love him with "all" yourself? The implications are significant. Jesus taught this love is the greatest of all God's commands in his law. Today, as you do your job, interact with family and friends and use your spiritual gifts in the life of your church, how can you do those things in a way that expresses your wholehearted love for God?

A prayer expressing your love for God
"Father in heaven, my love for you knows no bounds. I love you with my entire being. Help me today to express that love through my words and actions, to align my life with that love Jesus called your greatest command. As an expression of my love for you, let me love others with Jesus' love: my family, coworkers, neighbors and brothers and sisters in Christ. Help me cling to that love when things go wrong today, when difficulties arise. Teach me, God, to love as you loved us when you gave your Son as our Savior and King. To the praise of your name, amen."

To read more of God's word
Deuteronomy 6, Psalm 36, II Thessalonians 3:1-5

Write a personal response to the King's Agenda

DAY 7

Ask the One who said,
"Love your neighbor as yourself."

Luke 10:25-37
And behold, a lawyer stood up to put him to the test, saying, "Teacher, what shall I do to inherit eternal life?" ²⁶ He said to him, "What is written in the Law? How do you read it?" ²⁷ And he answered, "You shall love the Lord your God with all your heart and with all your soul and with all your strength and with all your mind, and your neighbor as yourself." ²⁸ And he said to him, "You have answered correctly; do this, and you will live."

But he, desiring to justify himself, said to Jesus, "And who is my neighbor?" ³⁰ Jesus replied, "A man was going down from Jerusalem to Jericho, and he fell among robbers, who stripped him and beat him and departed, leaving him half dead. ³¹ Now by chance a priest was going down that road, and when he saw him he passed by on the other side. ³² So likewise a Levite, when he came to the place and saw him, passed by on the other side. ³³ But a Samaritan, as he journeyed, came to where he was, and when he saw him, he had compassion. ³⁴ He went to him and bound up his wounds, pouring on oil and wine. Then he set him on his own animal and brought him to an inn and took care of him. ³⁵ And the next day he took out two denarii and gave them to the innkeeper, saying, 'Take care of him, and whatever more you spend, I will repay you when I come back.' ³⁶ Which of these three, do you think, proved to be a neighbor to the man who fell among the robbers?" ³⁷ He said, "The one who showed him mercy." And Jesus said to him, "You go, and do likewise."

Notice
One expression of our wholehearted love for God is that we love our neighbor. In Dr. Luke's account of this command, the lawyer famously asks Jesus, "And who is my neighbor?" In answer, Jesus tells one of his most famous parables, The Good Samaritan. The priest passed by the needy man, as did the worship leader, but the Samaritan stopped to aid him at his own expense and time. To love our neighbor is to stop what we are doing and go to some trouble to intervene to provide practical assistance. It is showing mercy. God has been merciful to us, and we in turn show our neighbors mercy. This is the second greatest of God's commands.

Think about it
One distinguishing mark of modern life is a hectic schedule. "I'm too busy" is a repeated phrase. We've all said it many times. Are we too busy to love others? To stop what we are doing and show the mercy of Jesus to someone in need? Consider your day today: Is there room in your to-do list for love, for practical kindness and generosity, to show God's love?

A prayer of willingness to love others by God's grace
"My Father, you have made clear to me in your word that I am called to love: to love you first and foremost, to love my neighbors, to love my fellow believers, even to love my enemies. God, please help me love my neighbor today. Open a door for me to make a difference in someone's life. Don't let me miss an open window of opportunity. Prompt me by your Holy Spirit and give me wisdom in how best to respond. I want to be your vessel of love today and every day, by your grace and for your glory, amen."

To read more of God's word
Leviticus 19:9-17, I Corinthians 13

Write a personal response to the King's Agenda

Call upon the One who said, "Pray without ceasing."

Luke 18:1-8
And he told them a parable to the effect that they ought always to pray and not lose heart. [2] He said, "In a certain city there was a judge who neither feared God nor respected man. [3] And there was a widow in that city who kept coming to him and saying, 'Give me justice against my adversary.' [4] For a while he refused, but afterward he said to himself, 'Though I neither fear God nor respect man, [5] yet because this widow keeps bothering me, I will give her justice, so that she will not beat me down by her continual coming.'" [6] And the Lord said, "Hear what the unrighteous judge says. [7] And will not God give justice to his elect, who cry to him day and night? Will he delay long over them? [8] I tell you, he will give justice to them speedily. Nevertheless, when the Son of Man comes, will he find faith on earth?"

Notice
What a vivid parable. It involves a corrupt judge ("neither feared God nor respected man") and an "importunate" widow. We don't use that word much anymore, but it means "troublesome persistence." The judge assumed if he refused to help her, she would just go away. He didn't reckon on her troublesome persistence. She refused to take no for an answer, and eventually the judge gave her justice in her case. The point is NOT that God is like this judge. Rather, the point of the parable is, are we like this widow? Are we willing to persevere in prayer and not lose heart? Verse 8 makes clear that persistence in prayer takes faith.

Think about it
When we bring our requests to God, he often says yes, sometimes no and at times he makes us wait. God asks us to trust him — to trust his wisdom in giving us what is best and to trust his timing for the when. We are often impatient. We want what we want when we want it, and we want it now. But our Father's wisdom and timing are impeccable. The question is will we trust him and keep on praying and rest in his goodness? Will we "always pray and not lose heart"?

A prayer for perseverance in prayer
"God my Father, forgive me for being so impatient and for treating you more like a butler than a loving father. Teach me all the good lessons of waiting. Help me to trust you with my whole heart and lean not on my own way of figuring everything out. Thank you for saying yes, but thank you also for the times you have said no in your infinite wisdom. By your Holy Spirit, help me to always pray and not lose heart, to persevere in both faith and prayer and trust you completely without reservation. In my Savior's name, amen.

To read more of God's word
Isaiah 40, Proverbs 3:5-6, Romans 11:33-36

Write a personal response to the King's Agenda

DAY 9

Trust the One who said, "Don't be anxious."

Matthew 6:25-34
"Therefore I tell you, do not be anxious about your life, what you will eat or what you will drink, nor about your body, what you will put on. Is not life more than food, and the body more than clothing? [26] Look at the birds of the air: they neither sow nor reap nor gather into barns, and yet your heavenly Father feeds them. Are you not of more value than they? [27] And which of you by being anxious can add a single hour to his span of life? [28] And why are you anxious about clothing? Consider the lilies of the field, how they grow: they neither toil nor spin, [29] yet I tell you, even Solomon in all his glory was not arrayed like one of these. [30] But if God so clothes the grass of the field, which today is alive and tomorrow is thrown into the oven, will he not much more clothe you, O you of little faith? [31] Therefore do not be anxious, saying, 'What shall we eat?' or 'What shall we drink?' or 'What shall we wear?' [32] For the Gentiles seek after all these things, and your heavenly Father knows that you need them all. [33] But seek first the kingdom of God and his righteousness, and all these things will be added to you.

[34] "Therefore do not be anxious about tomorrow, for tomorrow will be anxious for itself. Sufficient for the day is its own trouble."

Notice
King Jesus, the Master Teacher, shows once again the brilliant simplicity with which he communicates profound truth. Isn't life of greater value than externals like food and clothes? Yes, it is. He speaks in such relatable concepts: birds of the air, lilies of the field. We stop and think: Can our anxiety add a day to our life? An hour? No, it cannot. And it's foolishness. We have a heavenly Father who takes care of us. He can feed the birds and clothe the lilies (better than King Solomon), and so he will take care of us as we trust in him.

Think about it
The distress of anxiety and its companion worry is common. We all struggle with this from time to time. Jesus says, "Rather than worry about the everyday things that I will take care of, seek first my kingdom and righteousness. Leave the rest to me." How is your anxiety level today? What is worrying you? Jot down a few thoughts. Then bring them to the throne of grace in prayer.

A prayer of trusting God
"My heavenly Father, just as you feed the birds and clothe the living things in my garden, so you will take care of me. Thank you. I put all my trust in you. I release to you the things that cause me distress and fear. Rather than worry, I trust you to take care of them in your time and in your gracious way. I also pray for others in my family and church who struggle with fear and anxiety (perhaps name them to the Lord). My hope is in you, Maker of heaven and earth. I submit my life to your loving lordship. In Jesus' name, amen."

To read more of God's word
Genesis 22, Psalm 23, Philippians 4

Write your personal response to the King's Agenda

Cry out to the One who said, "Love your enemies."

Matthew 5:43-46
"You have heard that it was said, 'You shall love your neighbor and hate your enemy.' ⁴⁴ But I say to you, Love your enemies and pray for those who persecute you, ⁴⁵ so that you may be sons of your Father who is in heaven. For he makes his sun rise on the evil and on the good, and sends rain on the just and on the unjust. ⁴⁶ For if you love those who love you, what reward do you have? Do not even the tax collectors do the same?"

Notice
This is King Jesus teaching at his radical best. Most people love their friends and hate their enemies. Jesus says, "Love your enemies. Pray for them." Have you prayed for your enemies today? Why pray for them? Because, as verse 45 makes clear, God is able to save them. They may well become children of God. You might stand side-by-side with them at the Father's throne in his kingdom someday. Pray toward that end. Jesus says love them with a love that stands out from the crowd; love them with the love of King Jesus.

Think about it
Persecution is a daily reality for Christians all over the world. Harsh treatment of believers is neither "back then" or "soon" — it is now in Asia, the Middle East, parts of Africa and, yes, it might even be a reality for you in your workplace, neighborhood or extended family. Can you imagine praying for your persecutors from your prison cell? The Apostle Paul did just that. And Jesus prayed from the cross, "Father, forgive them...."

A prayer for our enemies in the name of our King
"Creator and Sustainer of the Universe, I am amazed King Jesus calls me to pray for my enemies. What radical love that is. Teach me that kind of love; teach me the love Jesus displayed from the cross. I pray today for those who are persecuting believers around the world. Give the Christians divine endurance and eternal hope and move mightily to save those who are hateful. I pray for those who are making my life difficult; save them, O God. Help me love them. You showed me such grand love, Father. Now let me show that love to those who need you. In Jesus' name, amen."

To read more of God's word
Genesis 39-41, Philippians 1, Philemon

Write a personal response to the King's Agenda

Obey the One who said,
"Blessed rather are those who hear the word of God and keep it."

Luke 11:27-28
As he said these things, a woman in the crowd raised her voice and said to him, "Blessed is the womb that bore you, and the breasts at which you nursed." [28] *But he said, "Blessed rather are those who hear the word of God and keep it."*

Notice
What a fascinating statement this "woman in the crowd" makes. She certainly recognized something unique and remarkable about Jesus and so honors his mother with a blessing. However, Jesus turns the situation around. Rather than "blessing" his mother, he points the woman (and the surrounding crowd) to the "blessing" of those who hear the commands of God and obey them. Perhaps this statement of King Jesus inspired James to write in his epistle, "But be doers of the word and not hearers only, deceiving yourselves" (James 1:22). Who are blessed by God? Those who hear God's commands and align their lives with that teaching by being "doers" of the word — those who walk in obedience of faith.

Think about it
If this is the blessed life, to obey God's commands, then it makes sense to hear the commands of King Jesus and pray them back to him. That's exactly what we are doing these 21 Days of Focused Prayer. We are responding to the commands of our Master by talking to the Father about them. Included in prayer is our willingness to submit ourselves to what he instructs, to align our lives to those commands. Anything less is hypocrisy and disobedience: I hear what you're saying, Lord, but don't expect me to do anything in response. Jesus here calls us to the blessed life, the happy life, of kingdom living — aligning our lives with the King's Agenda.

A prayer offering our obedience to our King
"Father in heaven, today I hear the voice of Jesus telling me to walk in obedience of faith. Help me, God. I want to be an obedient servant. I want to live my life in alignment with King Jesus. Help me be a doer of the word and not just a hearer. Please help me reject hypocrisy and embrace obedience. Guide me today by your Holy Spirit. May every decision I make today be in healthy alignment with your instructions in Scripture. Help me to walk in love today, the greatest and second commands. I love you, Father, and ask you to enable me to love my neighbors. In fact, help me love my enemies as well.

What I pray for myself I pray also for my family and church
Father, grant us today the grace to walk faithfully in obedience to the King's Agenda. I submit myself to you. In Jesus' name, amen."

To read more of God's word
Psalm 119, James 1

Write a personal response to the King's Agenda

Exalt the One who said, "Worship in spirit and in truth."

John 4:23-26
"But the hour is coming, and is now here, when the true worshipers will worship the Father in spirit and truth, for the Father is seeking such people to worship him. ²⁴ God is spirit, and those who worship him must worship in spirit and truth." ²⁵ The woman said to him, "I know that Messiah is coming (he who is called Christ). When he comes, he will tell us all things." ²⁶ Jesus said to her, "I who speak to you am he."

Notice
On a journey to Galilee, Jesus goes through Samaria and travels a road of great historic (Jacob's well) and religious significance. Remarkably, Jesus asks a Samaritan woman for a drink of water from the well and turns it into a life-changing conversation about Living Water. Included is this insight about true worship: both spirit (emotion, heart) and truth (intellect, mind). The woman says, in effect, "I know some day the Messiah will tell us what we need to know." And King Jesus reveals himself to her, "I who speak to you am he." Imagine how her pulse must have raced. The Christ was calling her to trust in him (the Living Water) and to follow him as a wholehearted worshiper.

Think about it
Worship is the full engagement of the Christ-follower in honoring and glorifying God. It is not a matter of location or of style, but of heart and mind. Worship is far more than the music time in our "service" (though God gave us music as one vital way to express this "heart and mind" full engagement). Worship is an all-of-life response to our King Jesus, both personal and gathered with other believers, in which we offer ourselves wholly to him. Worship is not one hour a week. It is our week. Are you a worshiper? Is your worship an offering of yourself completely to God, heart and mind, through the Living Water, King Jesus?

A prayer exalting the One who called us to worship in spirit and truth
"What a privilege to exalt you, heavenly Father, Maker of heaven and earth, Author of our salvation. I praise you for your gift of Living Water, your Son, my Lord Jesus Christ. I delight in that gift and drink deeply today of that Water. I offer you today my entire self, heart and mind, emotions and intellect. I place my life before you. Cleanse me; fill me; use me as your vessel, O God. May my day today be invested in exalting Jesus Christ, however and wherever you give me opportunity. May my life be a prayer of praise to you today, Father, and as a result may others look to the Living Water. For the honor and glory of Jesus Christ, amen."

To read more of God's word
Psalm 145, John 4

Write a personal response to the King's Agenda

Submit to the One who said, "Lay up treasures in heaven."

Matthew 6:19-21
"Do not lay up for yourselves treasures on earth, where moth and rust destroy and where thieves break in and steal, [20] but lay up for yourselves treasures in heaven, where neither moth nor rust destroys and where thieves do not break in and steal. [21] For where your treasure is, there your heart will be also."

Notice
The practical, down-to-earth teaching of King Jesus once again grabs our attention. Even Jesus knew about moth-eaten clothes, a rusty bucket and stolen sheep. His instruction "lived" in our world. His illustrations point us to a different kind of focus: instead of this world, focus on the next. Focus on the kingdom of God. Invest your treasures (time, talent, money) in those things that will outlast the great judgment fire of God to come. Invest in spreading the gospel of God. Invest in fulfilling the global purpose of God — the King's Agenda.

Think about it
We've all probably had the experience. Perhaps it was the first dent in a new(er) car, or the theft of a new laptop, or finding termites eating away at the house. Yikes! We are reminded again and again that the stuff of this world is not what lasts. King Jesus tells us to make eternal investments, for they cannot fade. How can we invest in the King's Agenda? Buying lunch to build friendship with our neighbor who needs the Lord; supporting our missionary friends who are taking the gospel to unreached people groups; giving faithfully to our church to support its vital local ministry (like VBS, youth group, the local pregnancy help center, even our own staff — who are giving their lives to the King). Where is your treasure invested? Will those investments outlive this present world? Do they align with the kingdom?

A prayer of submission to Christ
Father, today I place my time, my abilities and my money in your divine hands. I submit them to you. In fact, I give my whole self to you. Guide me by your Spirit to invest myself in things that will last forever. Please, Lord, create in me a generous, giving heart and renew my kingdom focus. Help me live for your agenda and not my own or the world's. Give me discernment, so that my kingdom investments will really count and not be wasted. Father, I want to be a cheerful giver. May it be so in the name of Jesus, my King, amen."

To read more of God's word
Deuteronomy 12:1-12; II Corinthians 8-9; I Timothy 6:18

Write your personal response to the King's Agenda

DAY 14

Cry out to the One who said, "What God has joined together let no man separate."

Mark 10:2-9
And Pharisees came up and in order to test him asked, "Is it lawful for a man to divorce his wife?" [3] He answered them, "What did Moses command you?" [4] They said, "Moses allowed a man to write a certificate of divorce and to send her away." [5] And Jesus said to them, "Because of your hardness of heart he wrote you this commandment. [6] But from the beginning of creation, 'God made them male and female.' [7] Therefore a man shall leave his father and mother and hold fast to his wife, [8] and the two shall become one flesh. So they are no longer two but one flesh. [9] What therefore God has joined together, let not man separate."

Notice
There was a dispute among the rabbis regarding divorce, a discrepancy in their views. The Pharisees were in essence asking Jesus to side with one rabbi or another, to "show his hand" as to which rabbi he considered correct. Wisely, masterfully, teacher Jesus responds by going all the way back to Genesis and God's purpose in marriage. God's design was that a male and female leave their parents and "hold fast" for life, the two now one. Jesus clarifies, "You want to know my view on divorce? Hear what I say about marriage, 'What therefore God has joined together, let not man separate.'"

Think about it
Divorce is a painful subject for many of us. So many families have been impacted. Yet, if the church of Jesus Christ does not take a stand for the permanence of marriage, who will? We do so not to hurt those who have been traumatized by divorce, but to honor the Master Designer and trust in his plan for the family and society and the church. Certainly, even in the pain we or those we love have experienced, we can pray for marriages. And we can call upon God for his sustaining grace. We can set an example of long-term commitment, enduring love, faithfulness and fidelity. If you know of a friend or family member whose marriage is difficult and painful, pray for them. Pray also for the marriages of leaders in your church family. Our enemy often attacks on that front. God help us.

Crying out for marriages
"O God, I cry out to you today on behalf of married couples. Sustain them by your grace and the Holy Spirit, O Lord. I pray for my own marriage (if married), as well as those of my family and church family. How we need your help, Father. Help us model in our marriages the relationship between Christ and the church — what a tall order that is. Help husbands to love their wives and wives to respect their husbands. May our church be a shelter for those who need help with marriage and family life. And may we support the hurting. I pray for the marriage of my pastor(s) and other church leaders, Father. Protect them from any harm the evil one would plot to do against them. And what I pray for them I pray for myself. In Jesus' name, amen."

To read more of God's word
Genesis 2, Ephesians 5, I Corinthians 13

Write your personal response to the King's Agenda

Cry out to the One who said,
"Render to Caesar the things that are Caesar's."

Mark 12:13-17
And they sent to him some of the Pharisees and some of the Herodians, to trap him in his talk. [14] And they came and said to him, "Teacher, we know that you are true and do not care about anyone's opinion. For you are not swayed by appearances, but truly teach the way of God. Is it lawful to pay taxes to Caesar, or not? Should we pay them, or should we not?" [15] But, knowing their hypocrisy, he said to them, "Why put me to the test? Bring me a denarius and let me look at it." [16] And they brought one. And he said to them, "Whose likeness and inscription is this?" They said to him, "Caesar's." [17] Jesus said to them, "Render to Caesar the things that are Caesar's, and to God the things that are God's." And they marveled at him.

Notice
It is never a good idea to try to trap King Jesus. But that's what certain religious leaders tried to do, first feigning respect, then offering their zinger question about taxes to Caesar. Zealots opposed paying tax to Rome; Herodians and others cooperated with Rome to "go along and get along" for their own gain. The trap was set: Jesus is in trouble with somebody whichever way he goes on this one. Or so they thought. Jesus brilliantly answers with a question of his own, "Whose likeness is on the coin?" And then the remarkable statement, "Render to Caesar," effectively putting the ball very much back in the court of those who came to him.

Think about it
Two implications are immediately clear. We ought to exercise an appropriate citizenship in our country, paying taxes, obeying just laws, etc. Yet we also know our nation is needy, with sin rampant and rebellion a great offense to our holy God. Do we pray for our sin-sick nation? Then the second question — are we offering to God the things that belong to him? Do we generously give to the kingdom work of God? Do we use our spiritual gifts for the glory of God and the building up of the church? Do we pray fervently and earnestly for kingdom breakthroughs in church planting, missions and evangelism? Have we fully embraced the King's Agenda?

Crying out to Christ for our nation and his eternal kingdom .
"My heavenly Father and all-wise God, give me a healthy perspective on both my earthly citizenship and my heavenly one. I pray for our nation, asking you to do a grand work of grace in our land, a work of revival among your people and a work of renewal in our culture. Forgive us our many sins, break our rebellious attitude, turn our nation from darkness to light, O God. And then, Father, I give myself wholly to you for the building up of your church. Help me also to be a solid kingdom citizen. Give me a spirit of generosity, a desire to use my gifts for you and a heart that longs for Christ to be magnified in my life. Fill me with your Holy Spirit. I surrender myself to you. In Jesus' name, amen."

To read more of God's word
Psalm 33, Romans 13

Write your personal response to the King's Agenda

DAY 16

Declare the glory of the One who said, "I and the Father are one."

John 10:22-30
At that time the Feast of Dedication took place at Jerusalem. It was winter, 23 and Jesus was walking in the temple, in the colonnade of Solomon. 24 So the Jews gathered around him and said to him, "How long will you keep us in suspense? If you are the Christ, tell us plainly." 25 Jesus answered them, "I told you, and you do not believe. The works that I do in my Father's name bear witness about me, 26 but you do not believe because you are not among my sheep. 27 My sheep hear my voice, and I know them, and they follow me. 28 I give them eternal life, and they will never perish, and no one will snatch them out of my hand. 29 My Father, who has given them to me, is greater than all, and no one is able to snatch them out of the Father's hand. 30 I and the Father are one."

Notice
With great clarity here, Jesus declares his deity as the second person of the trinity. "I and the Father are one." Jewish religious leaders demand to know if Jesus is the Christ, that is, the Messiah promised in the Hebrew Bible. "Tell us plainly." Jesus cites several layers of evidence: 1) I have already told you. 2) The works I do in my Father's name bear witness. 3) My sheep hear my voice and follow me. To these I give eternal life, they will never perish and no one can snatch them from me. My Father, greater than all, certainly can hold on to them without fail. What a grand truth. Jesus is the Messiah and believers in Christ have heard his voice and followed him, and they cannot be snatched away by the enemy.

Think about it
If you are a believer in Jesus Christ, your Savior is in fact the Son of God and promised Deliverer. He declared it to be so in the Gospels; he revealed it through his miracles and signs, as recorded in the Gospels; and he graciously spoke to you through the gospel and allowed you to hear his voice and follow him. This is saving grace. Jesus and his heavenly Father have a strong grip on you, and they won't ever let go. As you read the word and pray today, hear his voice, know the King's Agenda and follow him. Tomorrow, too. The life of a Jesus disciple is one of trusting, taking in his word, "hearing" what his word has to say and following in obedience. That's why it's good to pray the King's Agenda.

A prayer of praise to God the Son
"What an extraordinary gift, Father, you have given — your unique and only Son, Jesus. I praise him, Jesus my Lord and King, and exalt him as the true Messiah. I dedicate my life to declaring his glory, his love, his beauty and his salvation. May nothing ever surpass my love for Jesus Christ, and may I follow in the obedience of faith every day. May our church ever be devoted to singing the praises of Jesus. May we preach his gospel and kingly agenda, love you, our neighbors and enemies and participate in your grand kingdom plan, O God. Take my life, and let it be consecrated, Lord, to You. In Jesus' name, amen."

To read more of God's word
Exodus 20, Psalm 138, John 10

Write your personal response to the King's Agenda

DAY 17

Ask help of the One who said, "I will make you fishers of men."

Matthew 4:18-22
While walking by the Sea of Galilee, he saw two brothers, Simon (who is called Peter) and Andrew his brother, casting a net into the sea, for they were fishermen. [19] And he said to them, "Follow me, and I will make you fishers of men." [20] Immediately they left their nets and followed him. [21] And going on from there he saw two other brothers, James the son of Zebedee and John his brother, in the boat with Zebedee their father, mending their nets, and he called them. [22] Immediately they left the boat and their father and followed him.

Notice
We previously prayed about the command of King Jesus, "Follow me" (Day 2). Here in Matthew's Gospel that command has a promise attached, "I will make you fishers of men." To these experienced fishermen, Jesus was laying down a purpose-filled kingdom challenge: "Set your sights on fishing for people." Their response was immediate, and it was life-altering. How fascinating that Jesus would choose a group of fishermen to join him. How appropriate. Jesus embraces their way of life but kicks it up a few notches — "Let's find people to become part of my kingdom family." And that's just what happened, as the Book of Acts testifies.

Think about it
Does your life have such a purpose? Are you people fishing? Are you a witness to the gospel of Jesus Christ, telling others of his life-changing power? God can and will use you to declare his good news to people in your sphere of influence, if you are faithful, available and teachable. Ponder this: You might be the first genuine, Christ-loving, Spirit-filled believer the barista has ever met. Your neighbor has seen that your life is different. Have you told him or her that following Jesus is the reason? That your ready smile is because your sins are forgiven, your hope has been set on fire and you have the love of Jesus in your heart? Do you pray for the salvation of those in your sphere of influence?

Before you pray, make a list of five people in your sphere of life who need Jesus. Let's call it your "fishing list five," OK?

1. _____
2. _____
3. _____
4. _____
5. _____

A prayer asking for God's help in "fishing" for people who need to know him
"What a privilege, Father, to tell others what Jesus Christ has done for me. I want to be 'on mission' with the King's Agenda to grow your kingdom family, life-by-life, household-by-household. Today I ask you to take out these five hearts of stone and replace them with new hearts of flesh that beat for you (pray for each person on your "fishing list five"). Open windows of opportunity for me to share the gospel today, Father. Help me to be led by your Holy Spirit. And thank you for saving me. Thank you for giving me the great gift of salvation by faith in Jesus Christ, my Savior/King, amen."

To read more of God's word
Ezekiel 36:22-38, Acts 26, Romans 10:1-17

Write your personal response to the King's Agenda

Call upon the One who said, "Make disciples of all nations."

Matthew 28:16-20
Now the eleven disciples went to Galilee, to the mountain to which Jesus had directed them. [17] And when they saw him they worshiped him, but some doubted. [18] And Jesus came and said to them, "All authority in heaven and on earth has been given to me. [19] Go therefore and make disciples of all nations, baptizing them in the name of the Father and of the Son and of the Holy Spirit, [20] teaching them to observe all that I have commanded you. And behold, I am with you always, to the end of the age."

Notice
This is often called the Great Commission, and it is packed with meaning. The risen Christ first establishes his authority — he has every right to commission his disciples this way. Then he commissions his disciples to make disciples by proclaiming the good news of Jesus Christ. That's the verb, or command, in the Commission. Making disciples involves going to all nations (ethne, or people groups), baptizing them when they begin to follow Jesus and teaching them the agenda of King Jesus (all he has commanded). The Commission ends with a fabulous promise: I will always be with you as you fulfill this Commission I have given you.

Think about it
The Great Commission initiated by Jesus Christ himself is still in effect. We have this same calling, to take the good news of Jesus Christ to all the ethnic and language "peoples" of our planet. It's a full-orbed vision involving going and sending, telling, baptizing (immersing in water new converts to Christ as a public profession of their new faith) and teaching the King's Agenda. Making disciples is our highest and grandest calling as the church. It fuels our passion as a movement to plant healthy, vibrant, reproducing churches in every people group on earth. Are you personally "on board" with this Commission? Are you doing your part?

Before you pray
We recommend "adopting" an unreached people group for your ongoing intercession. Do you know of one, through your church perhaps? If you don't, ask a pastor or missions leader at your church and commit to regular prayer for that unique people group.

Calling upon God for help in reaching all the peoples of the earth
"What a grand vision you have, heavenly Father, for filling the earth with worshipers from every language and ethnic group. No people are left out; none is excluded. I commit myself to being part of your Great Commission force, Lord, for the fulfilling of the King's Agenda to make disciples. Help me to live 'on mission' and to either go or send others. Bless my church's efforts to fulfill our fair share of this Commission. In particular, I pray for the _____ people, that a church would be planted among them and many among them would embrace Jesus Christ as Lord and Savior, amen."

To read more of God's word
Genesis 12:1-3, Isaiah 25, Psalm 117, Revelation 7:9-17

Write your personal response to the King's Agenda

Call upon the One who said, "You will be my witnesses."

Acts 1:6-9
So when they had come together, they asked him, "Lord, will you at this time restore the kingdom to Israel?" *7* He said to them, "It is not for you to know times or seasons that the Father has fixed by his own authority. *8* But you will receive power when the Holy Spirit has come upon you, and you will be my witnesses in Jerusalem and in all Judea and Samaria, and to the end of the earth." *9* And when he had said these things, as they were looking on, he was lifted up, and a cloud took him out of their sight.

Notice
King Jesus has risen from the dead and now appears to his disciples. With the Messiah risen, it must be the kingdom will be restored to Israel now, right? But that is not God's plan. He has another plan, and it involves us. "Don't be fixated on times and seasons for such things; God has those in hand. But here's what will happen — you will receive power from the Spirit of God, and you will be my witnesses here, there and everywhere." They inquired about overthrowing Rome and restoring Israel to its rightful place. King Jesus answered with a key piece of God's agenda: the followers of Jesus bearing gospel witness to the religious center of Judaism (Jerusalem), to the nearby ethnic centers (Judea, Samaria) and, in fact, to the entire earth (all the peoples).

Think about it
What Jesus declared to his disciples then, we are still fulfilling now. We have the amazing gift of God's Spirit dwelling in us and filling us. We have our divine calling to be witnesses to King Jesus. There is much gospel ground to be taken. There are unreached people groups who still do not have a reasonable number of believers to reach their own language or ethnic group with the gospel. And there are unengaged, unreached people groups. These are not only unreached, but as of yet they are not even engaged by potential witnesses (such as missionaries or nearby evangelistic witnesses). Mark 13:10 says, "And the gospel must first be proclaimed to all nations."

Calling upon the Lord for help in witnessing
"Father, because I love you so much and am so thankful for all you have done for me in Jesus Christ, it is my delight and desire to be a witness to others. Help me speak the truth of the gospel, share what Christ has done for me and show the love of Jesus wherever you send me. I am willing to go, to live "on mission," to do my part as a "goer" or a "sender" so that the Great Commission is fulfilled. I pray again for the unreached people group, the _____ (from yesterday's reading), that they would hear of Jesus Christ, of the cross, resurrection and saving faith in Christ and be saved. Thank you for the joy of being part of this global gospel revolution, Father. In Jesus' name, amen."

To read more of God's word
Isaiah 56:1-8, Luke 24:36-53, Romans 15:15-33

Write your personal response to the King's Agenda

Follow the One who said,
"I am the way, the truth and the life."

John 14:1-6
"Let not your hearts be troubled. Believe in God; believe also in me. ² In my Father's house are many rooms. If it were not so, would I have told you that I go to prepare a place for you? ³ And if I go and prepare a place for you, I will come again and will take you to myself, that where I am you may be also. ⁴ And you know the way to where I am going." ⁵ Thomas said to him, "Lord, we do not know where you are going. How can we know the way?" ⁶ Jesus said to him, "I am the way, and the truth, and the life. No one comes to the Father except through me."

Notice
On the road to the cross, in the upper room, Jesus offers great reassurance and hope to his disciples — and to us. Don't be troubled by the events that are unfolding. Instead, believe in my Father and believe in me. You will have a future dwelling place with me that will last forever. Thomas' question opens the door for one of the grandest of all of Jesus' statements: "I am the way, and the truth, and the life." Jesus is our way to eternal life with our heavenly Father. Jesus, the author and perfecter of our faith, is also the grand object of it.

Think about it
Do we need a road map to know where we're going? Jesus is the way. Do we need a standard of truth for this mixed-up world of situational ethics and political correctness? Jesus is the truth. Do we need to know how to experience life to its fullest, with enduring joy now and forever? Jesus is the life. A massive amount of information and misinformation is available to us every moment of every day. It's one click away. But does it provide clarity? Does it provide true guidance? Does it reveal the King's Agenda? Most of it does not. King Jesus is the way, the truth and the life. No one finds fellowship with God the Father except through him.

A prayer for followers of Jesus
"Holy and eternal God, giver of life and breath and every good thing, I come to you today with a heart full of thanksgiving that you have shown me the way through your only, unique Son, Jesus. I put my faith and full confidence in him as the only way to eternal life with you. I look to Jesus as my road map for daily living, standard of truth and source of true joy. Help me this day, Father, to point others to Jesus. Give me words to testify to the difference Jesus Christ has made in my life and to the profound truth of the gospel. Fill me today with your Holy Spirit. And may our church be a lighthouse of faith, hope and love in our community as we point to King Jesus as the way, the truth and the life. In his matchless name, the name above every name, amen."

To read more of God's word
I Chronicles 16, John 14, Philippians 1

Write your personal response to the King's Agenda

Exalt the One who will come as "King of kings and Lord of lords."

Revelation 19:11-16
Then I saw heaven opened, and behold, a white horse. The one sitting on it is called Faithful and True, and in righteousness he judges and makes war. ¹² His eyes are like a flame of fire, and on his head are many diadems, and he has a name written that no one knows but himself. ¹³ He is clothed in a robe dipped in blood, and the name by which he is called is The Word of God. ¹⁴ And the armies of heaven, arrayed in fine linen, white and pure, were following him on white horses. ¹⁵ From his mouth comes a sharp sword with which to strike down the nations, and he will rule them with a rod of iron. He will tread the winepress of the fury of the wrath of God the Almighty. ¹⁶ On his robe and on his thigh he has a name written, King of kings and Lord of lords.

Notice
We return on the 21st day to where we began in the introduction. The Scriptures reveal Jesus to be the one and only "King of kings and Lord of lords." The King's Agenda is the agenda of Jesus Christ our Lord. What Jesus reveals about himself we believe as truth; what he commands we obey, trusting his way is the path to joy, purpose, hope and love. The white horse represents the victory of the conquering hero — Jesus Christ. His character? Faithful and true and righteous. Is he truly a King? The King? Well, he wears on his head many diadems; he is clothed with a kingly robe, dipped in the blood of the cross; his name is the Word of God; and he is followed by the mighty army of heaven. Will our King be a judge? Oh yes, from his mouth comes a sharp sword, and he will execute the wrath of Almighty God on the nations.

Think about it
Jesus is King of kings and Lord of lords. His commands are our agenda, and he wills us to obey them, not from some capricious, volatile temper, but for our eternal hope and joy. Jesus knows what is best. He is leading us to an amazing life that will last forever, in his presence, where there will be fullness of joy and pleasures forevermore (Psalm 16:11 — worth memorizing). And so we commend to you, every day, the wisdom of praying the King's Agenda. When you align your prayers and your life with all Jesus taught, you choose to follow your Savior as a disciple who learns all his Master teaches and obeys him (Matthew 28:20). God bless you in this amazing journey as a disciple of King Jesus.

A prayer exalting God the Father and God the Son
"O God of Creation, God of Salvation, God of Eternity — today I exalt you as the only True and Living God. And I thank you for Jesus, my Savior, who is King of kings and Lord of lords. I thank you for the Scriptures, which show me the path of life and the agenda of Jesus. Help me to follow wisely, Father. Fill me today with your Holy Spirit, so that I can follow Jesus effectively. I offer every part of me to King Jesus: my lips to praise and bear witness, my hands to love as Christ loved, my feet to go where you want me to go, my mind to believe and obey and my heart to know and love Jesus more. In his holy and magnificent name, amen."

To read more of God's word
Isaiah 66:1-2, Psalm 150, Revelation 21-22

Write your final response to the King's Agenda

ABOUT

About the author
Dana Olson recently completed his 36th year in full-time Christian ministry, all with Converge. For more than 26 years he led prayer mobilization for Converge, first chairing a prayer commission and later serving as director of Prayer First. He has preached and taught on prayer in hundreds of churches across America and led prayer journeys to our international mission fields. He has also provided prayer opportunities for pastors, missionaries, chaplains and others from coast to coast. He is currently senior pastor for Preaching and Vision at Faith Baptist Fellowship, a multisite church in Sioux Falls, South Dakota. He also serves on America's National Prayer Committee and is chairman emeritus of the Denominational Prayer Leaders Network. Dana and Christa have three adult daughters, Anna (the gentle soul), Mary (the missionary) and Betsy (the physicist).

Who is Converge?
Converge is a movement of churches working to help people meet, know and follow Jesus. We do this by starting and strengthening churches together worldwide. For over 165 years we've helped churches bring life change to communities in the U.S. and around the world through church planting and multiplication, leadership training and global missions.

Learn more at converge.org

Made in the USA
Middletown, DE
07 January 2020